P.O. Box 238
Morley, MO 63767
(573) 472-9800
www.acclaimpress.com

Book & Cover Design: Rodney Atchley

ISBN: 978-1-956027-56-3 / 1-956027-56-4
Library of Congress Control Number: 2023935514

First Printing: 2023
Printed in the United States of America
10 9 8 7 6 5 4 3 2 1

This publication was produced using available information.
The publisher regrets it cannot assume responsibility for errors or omissions.

CONTENTS

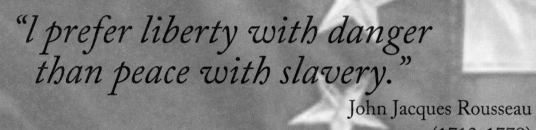

"I prefer liberty with danger
than peace with slavery."

John Jacques Rousseau
(1712-1778)

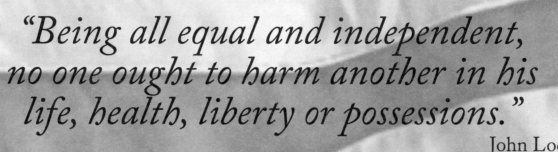

"*Being all equal and independent,
no one ought to harm another in his
life, health, liberty or possessions.*"

John Locke
(1632-1704)

FOREWORD

From April 15, 1996 to March 26, 1998, I served on the Bowling Green-Warren County Bicentennial Commission and was Chairman of the Research and Resources Committee*. Obviously, everyone realized that our county was named for someone named Warren, and a few even knew his name was Joseph Warren. However, only a handful of people knew that he was an outstanding physician, as well as a courageous revolutionary leader. At that time, I compiled a very brief biographical/historical sketch about him.

Recently, while searching for an idea for a paper to present to my literary club EQB**, I decided to expand the brief paper written in 1998, about Dr. Warren to include more personal and historical information. Kentucky was, after all, the fourth of twelve states to name a county (1796) for Major General Joseph Warren, M.D. I sincerely hope that the readers will find this material both interesting and informative.

Jerry W. Martin, M.D.

*All materials gathered were placed in the Kentucky Library Archives at WKU.
**EQB, or Ecce Quam Bonum: "Behold, how good", the beginning of the first verse of the 133rd Psalm.

"*The mistress we court is liberty; and it is better to die than to not attain her.*"[1]
—Dr. Joseph Warren, June 15, 1774

MAJOR GENERAL
JOSEPH WARREN, M.D.

June 11, 1741 - June 17, 1775

"Dulce et decorum pro patria mori."[2]

"The name of Joseph Warren is one of the most conspicuous in the annals of the Revolution. His memory is cherished with even warmer regard than that of some others, who, from the greater length of their career, and the wider sphere in which they acted, may be supposed to have rendered more important services to the country. This distinction in his favor is owing in part to the chivalrous beauty of his character, which naturally excites a sympathetic glow in every feeling mind; and in part to that untimely but glorious fate, which consecrated him as the first distinguished martyr in the cause of independence and liberty."[3]

"For many Americans, 1776 is the seminal year in the nation — the year the founding fathers signed the Declaration of Independence, initiating one of the greatest revolutions in the modern world."[4] Many would argue, however, that the most significant moment toward an irreversible conflict with Great Britain occurred a little more than a year earlier on June 17, 1775, at Breed's Hill.

"Joseph Warren was one of the popular leaders of Boston during the early stage of the American Revolution. He grasped its basic idea of civil freedom, and [he] aimed to impress on the public mind its dignity and glory."[5] After ten years of devotion to the patriot cause, "...he rose to be the head of public affairs [both civil and military] in Massachusetts, and became one of the most prominent men in New England."[6]

An 1854 geneology[7] of the Warren family obtained by Richard Frothingham from John Collins Warren, M.D., a relative of Joseph Warren and a Bostonian Brahmin, indicates that the Warren ancestry can be traced back to William Warren, a Norman baron of Danish extraction. He accompanied William the Conqueror on his expedition to England; fought at the Battle of Hastings (A.D. 1066); was rewarded with riches from the Saxons; and won the confidence of the court to such a degree that when King William left England on a return visit to his native land, William Warren was appointed one of two guardians of the kingdom. "From this ancestry the Warrens are followed down through earls, knights, and commoners, to the period of the colonization of our county."[8]

The Warren family tree had "...branched off in England long before anyone set sail for Plymouth Plantation or the Massachusetts Bay Colony."[9] Richard Warren, who immigrated to Massachusetts on the Mayflower in 1620, was a distant cousin, but the first ancestor in Joseph Warren's patrilinear line to settle in North America was Peter Warren[10], whose name first appeared in Massachusetts' Suffolk County records.[11] He bought land

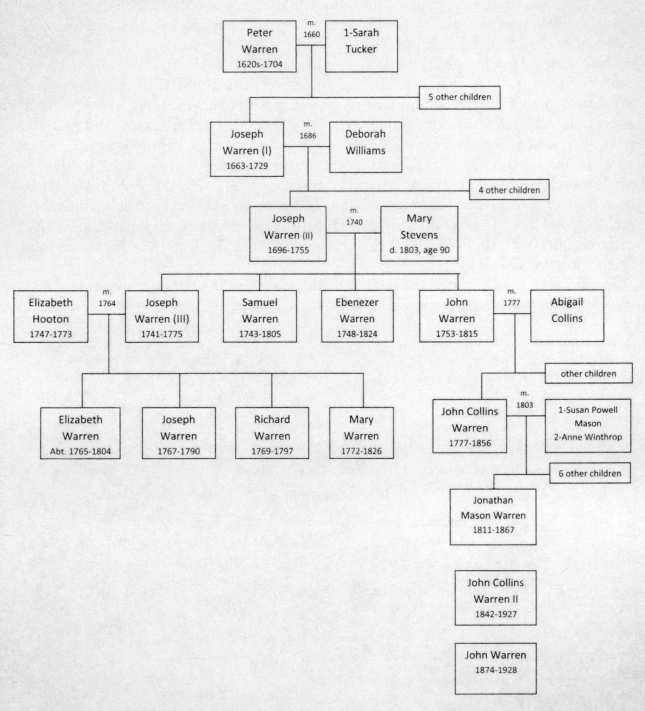

Genealogy of Joseph Warren, adapted from Rhoda Traux, The Doctors Warren of Boston – First Family of Surgery (Boston: Houghton Mifflin Company, 1968).

and settled on Essex Street (earlier called Auchmuty Lane) in Boston in March 1659. Peter married Sara Tucker (the daughter of Robert Tucker of Dorchester) in 1660, and they had eight children. After her death, he married Hannah, and they had three more children. After Hannah's death[12], he married his third wife Esther. He willed that Esther was to be granted a life estate that allowed her to live in the Essex Street house rent free for the remainder of her life. Peter died in 1704.

Peter's second son Joseph [I] was born on February 19, 1663. Joseph later married Deborah Williams[13] in 1686. They lived in the Essex Street house until 1714, when he sold the property[14] in order to buy a farm located in nearby Roxbury, which was a long walk or a short horseback ride down the narrow road along Boston's Neck, the only land route into town. Colonial inheritance laws followed the English practice of primogeniture, so this second son's inheritance of the Essex Street property implies that the elder brother had predeceased the father. Joseph Warren [I] died on July 13, 1729. Joseph Warren [II] had been born in 1669, and he later married Mary Stevens[15] on May 29, 1740. Joseph and Mary had four children, all boys. The oldest child Joseph [III] was born on June 11, 1741. Next came Samuel (Oct. 10, 1743-1805), then Ebenezer (Sept. 13, 1748-1824), and then John[16] "Jack" (July 14, 1753-1815).

Joseph [II] built a beautiful, three-story stone house[17] on the farm which was located on Braintree Road. The farm comprised many acres of pastures, woodlands, orchards, swamp-

Warren's eighteenth century family home in Roxbury, Massachusetts, sketch from the nineteenth century.

lands, and salt marshes. The orchards produced large numbers of russet apples.[18] They ripen in late October, taste best after a heavy frost, and keep throughout the winter, even as late as the following April or May. The apples' long shelf life made them ideal for local use over winter, as well as shipping on long voyages to Europe or the Caribbean. Their high sugar content rendered them very desirable for apple juice, hard cider, and apple butter.

A very traumatic and pivotal event occurred that had a significant impact on the Warren family:

> Roxbury, October 25, 1755. On Wednesday last a sorrowful accident happened here, as Mr. Joseph Warren [II], of this town was gathering apples from a tree, standing upon a ladder, at a considerable distance from the ground, he fell from thence, broke his neck, and expired in a few moments. He was an esteemed man of good standing, industrious, upright, honest and faithful; a serious exemplary Christian; a useful member of society; he was generally respected amongst us, and his death is universally lamented.[19]

"Joseph Warren's [III] rise from the son of a Roxbury farmer to a powerful gentleman revolutionary has remained buried beneath centuries of historical neglect."[20] He worked long, hard hours of intense manual labor on the farm from an early age: in the fields tending crops, raising a garden, working in the orchard, and delivering apples and milk to market. His parents were strong advocates of education, and they practiced a religion of Puritan standards based on Calvinist doctrine with a deep love and veneration of the Bible. His father (Joseph II) served as treasurer of the First (Congregationalist) Church in Roxbury and, in 1736, served on a building committee to construct a new meeting house, which was completed soon after Joseph's [III] birth. The first Great Awakening was raging along the eastern seaboard during the 1730s and '40s, led by evangelists like Jonathan Edwards, George Whitfield, William Cooper, and Samuel Cooper among many others.

He was significantly influenced by his father (Joseph II) who once told young Joseph that "I would rather have a son of mine dead than a coward." Joseph later told a younger brother that "...the recollection of that conversation, particularly the last sentiment in it expressed by his long departed father, thrilled in his memory and incited him to action."[21] That statement probably had a significant impact on him in the Battle of Breed's Hill.[22] After the Battles of Lexington and Concord, in response to British troops who scorned the provincials as cowards because they fired from concealed positions behind rocks, fences, and trees, an enraged Warren exclaimed, "These fellows say we won't fight: by heavens, I hope I shall die up to my knees in blood!"[23]

Joseph [III] attended four years at the Roxbury Latin School[24], which was modeled after grammar schools in England, and it served as a feeder institution to Harvard and other colleges. He had just started classes at Harvard (age 14) in mid-August 1755, and his father died in October. Tradition attributes his sponsorship at Harvard by Roxbury neighbors, which explains Joseph's postgraduate stint teaching at the Roxbury Latin School. It was common for a community to sponsor a promising student at college in expectation of their service teaching in community public grammar schools.[25]

At Harvard, he became proficient in rhetoric, mathematics, religion, and science, and exhibited competence in the Greek and Latin languages. He was recognized for his knowledge of chemistry, or the "...chymical aspects of natural philosophy."[26] He was a member of the debating club, which led to him improving his speaking skills. He enjoyed making points persuasively as well as engaging in verbal sparring and expressive improvisations. He was also a member of Marti-Mercurial militia group and, along with other physicians, was in the anatomical club, known as the Spunkers Club. He produced and directed Addison's historical drama, *Cato*, in his dorm suite on July 3, 1758.[27] Nathan Hale, as he approached his execution as a patriot spy, paraphrased Addison's Words, "What pity is it that we can die but once to serve our country!" Joseph was also inspired by Cato's Words and took them to heart when he said, "A day, an hour, of virtuous liberty is worth a whole eternity in bondage."[28]

While teaching at Roxbury Latin School, he furthered his postgraduate education by pursuing a Master of Arts degree in a manner typical of Harvard students at that time — through off-campus self-study and an oral dissertation delivered in Latin during graduation ceremonies. Warren argued against the proposition that all disease was caused by obstruction of bodily vessels as theorized by Dr. Boerhaave.[29] Warren discussed the pros and cons of his proposition versus the humeral idea of disease as expounded by medical physiologists of the day. A copy of his dissertation does not exist, so whatever he declared, the Harvard faculty accepted. Therefore, he was granted a Master of Arts degree in Medicine in 1762.

A year earlier, Joseph had started his apprenticeship under James Lloyd, M.D., one of Boston's most famous physicians. Dr. Lloyd had studied under the highly esteemed Boston physician John Clark, M.D. before traveling to London, where he trained at St. Guy's Hospital under the acclaimed surgeons William Cheselden, M.D. and Samuel Sharp, M.D. Dr. Lloyd returned to Boston in 1752, bringing his superior medical/surgical knowledge and training, and, throughout the 1750s, helped transform the practice of medicine in Boston.

Joseph Warren was a precocious student and "...was highly distinguished as a scholar..."[30] and had chosen his mentor wisely. He lived in the Lloyd home, quickly became acquainted with Dr. Lloyd's vast social network, and was suddenly thrust into and immersed within the highest realms of Boston society, a world beyond medicine. Warren quickly mastered the skill of a bedside manner and nuanced social interactions. In addition to learning how to run a successful practice, he learned how to com-

Edward Holyoke, Harvard's ninth president, by John Singleton Copley, ca. 1760.

port himself as an extension of his mentor's household. He learned proper social etiquette and improved his dress to achieve a more elegant appearance. Included in the two-year apprenticeship were guided readings in the basic sciences of medicine — anatomy, physiology, chemistry, pharmaceutical *materia medica* — as well as experience in diagnosis and treatment of both medical and surgical cases. Upon completion of training, the master would certify and recommend the physician/student as worthy of a practice of his own. Joseph was thusly designated in June 1763, at age 22.[31] "Dr. Lloyd had transformed Joseph Warren from an educated farm boy into a skilled and respected city physician."[32]

Joseph Warren joined the Masons as a young man. Their ethos coincided with his thinking and extended his circle of friends and acquaintances, both Whig and Tory. Boston's St. John's Modern Lodge was chartered July 30, 1733. St. Andrew's Lodge of Boston was chartered in the Scottish Ancient Rite on November 30, 1756. St. John's Lodge adopted a resolution in April 1761, forbidding all Masonic interactions with St. Andrew's Lodge. "It was into this environment of locally divided masonry

Warren's medical mentor, Dr. James Lloyd (1728–1810). From James Thatcher, American Medical Biography (Boston, 1828)

that Warren, then a medical apprentice, passed the first degree of Masonry at St. Andrew's Lodge."[33] He was voted a Fellow of the Craft on November 10, 1761, and at the next meeting on November 26th, he was admitted to full membership. His friend, silversmith Paul Revere, had been admitted the year before. Warren had to drop out of the lodge during the end of his apprenticeship, due to the establishment of his practice in 1763, and the small-pox epidemic of 1764. Dr. Warren was unanimously welcomed back in 1765. St. Andrew's Lodge elected Dr. Warren as their senior warden for 1766-67, and then elected him as their worshipful master in late 1767. Under his leadership, the St. Andrew's Lodge applied for and was granted the status of a Grand Lodge of Scottish Rite Ancients, and Warren became its Grand Master. The petition was signed by the Right Honorable George, Earl of Dalhousie on May 30, 1769. The charter and commission were in Secretary Paul Revere's possession by September 1769. In 1772, Lord Dumfries, successor to Lord Dalhousie as Grand Master of all Ancients, extended Warren's provincial jurisdiction from "...Boston, New England, and within 100 miles of same," to "...all of North America."[34] Warren missed only three meetings during his tenure as Grand Master from 1769 to 1775. Warren quickly became comfortable with the Masonic habits of secrecy. It is believed that some of his Masonic associates at St. Andrew's Lodge, disguised as Mohawk Indians, were participants in the Boston Tea Party.

Boarding British tea ships docked at Griffin's Wharf, Bostonians, thinly disguised as Native Americans, empty more than 300 chests of East India tea into the sea on December 15, 1774.

Joseph Warren, M.D. wrote numerous newspaper editorials concerning British abuses using assumed names: *Graph Iatoos*, the initials *B.W. Paskalos*, and *Philo Physic*. Those abuses were many: the Stamp Act, The Townshend Duties, the impoundment of John Hancock's ship *Liberty*, and the economic boycott of English imports among many other real or perceived threats of the British. In response to the capture of the *Liberty*, Joseph Quincy exclaimed, "We are the sons of Great Britain, not her bastards, and certainly not her slaves."[35] In reply, Joseph Warren said, "We will not concede to a position less than that of a true son, nor willingly submit to shackles, not as long as Puritan blood of our ancestors and their love for liberty still flows through our veins! Would to God this problem could be solved peacefully and quickly."[36]

After completing his medical training, he began his private medical/surgical practice in Roxbury. His practice grew rapidly, partially because of a smallpox epidemic. Warren worked endlessly to inoculate innumerable patients, even those who could not pay, causing someone to write, "...in the year 1764, when the small pox spread through Boston, and vast numbers were inoculated, he was among the physicians who were most eminent in the profession." Warren emerged as a new leader, a man "...in whom the people in the environs of Boston and Cambridge placed their highest confidence."[37] Joseph Warren, M.D., within just a few years, established one of the largest medical practices in Boston. In 1769, Thomas Young, M.D. claimed that Warren's practice was "now first in business in this town." He established himself as a caring and talented physician and gained much credibility among his fellow townsmen. He treated both Whig and Tory without prejudice.

Joseph Warren and Elizabeth Hooton were married on September 6, 1764. The local newspaper stated:

> Last Thursday Evening was married Doct. Joseph Warren, one of the Physicians of this Town, to Miss Betsy Hooton, only Daughter of the late Mr. Richard Hooton of this Town, Merchant, deceas'd, an accomplish'd young Lady with a hansome Fortun.[38]

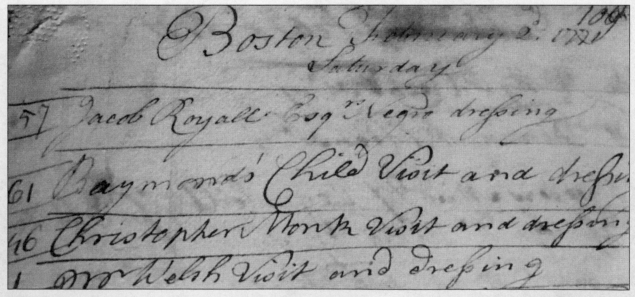

Warren's medical ledger entry for Christopher Monk, sixth victim of the Boston Massacre, 1771. (Massachusetts Historical Society)

Elizabeth Hooten Warren, by Henry Pelham. Museum of Fine Arts, Boston.

Joseph was twenty-three years old, and Elizabeth was eighteen years old. Her widowed father had passed away intestate at age thirty-seven on June 1, 1764, leaving her as his sole heir.[39] The ceremony was performed in the Congregational Church on Brattle Street in Boston[40], where both Joseph and Elizabeth were faithful members.[41] The wedding was conducted by the Rev. Samuel Cooper[42], who accepted a Portuguese coin in payment.

Massachusetts's initial charter had established the province as a self-governing private corporation. That status was revoked in 1691. The next year, a new, revised charter increased the governor's power, allowing Britain to exert greater political and military control over what was now a royal colony. No longer elected to office, the Governor General was now appointed directly by the Crown and assumed total command over the military. In October 1760, King George II passed away in the "34th year of his reign."[43] The Seven Years' War had caused the war debt to climb to over 120 million pounds.[44] The Massachusetts economy started sinking.

George II, whose reign marked the last time that an English king led his troops into battle. Painting by Thomas Hudson.

The price of food and firewood began rising, and as mentioned, the smallpox epidemic began on March 20, 1760.[45] A tremendously destructive fire consumed a portion of Boston in March. The blaze spread southeast from the center of town; the flames were visible for more than thirty miles and destroyed 350 homes and warehouses at a value of 100,000 to 300,000 pounds. The fire storm associated with the fire carried charred shingles, paper, and letters as far as Natasket, almost nine miles away.

In 1765, Writs of Assistance allowed customs officials to conduct arbitrary searches of homes and businesses in an attempt to mitigate the smuggling so rampant in port cities throughout the colonies. The holder of a writ could not be held responsible for any damage during the search. Many other unbearable burdens were placed on the people, such as: the Quartering Act, the Boston Port Act, the Currency Act, the Townshend Act, the Mas-

George III, King of Great Britain, 1738-1820

sachusetts Government and Administration of Justice Act, the Sugar Act, and the Coercive Act (Intolerable Act). These burdensome acts led to the Boston Tea Party, the Boston Massacre, the Battles at Lexington and Concord, and ultimately to the Battle at Breed's Hill and then open warfare which spread throughout all the other colonies.

In October 1765, Warren wrote to his friend and former Harvard classmate Edmund Dana — then in England studying medicine — about the Stamp Act:

Never has there been a time, since the first settlement of America, in which the people had so much reason as to be alarmed as the present. The whole continent is inflamed to the highest degree the colonies are now united for their defense against what they believe to be oppression.[46]

The British prime minister convinced the new king (George III) and Parliament to repeal the Stamp Act on March 18, 1766. In order to reaffirm their hegemony, Parliament passed the Declaratory Act to replace it, which reaffirmed British "...full power and authority to make laws and statutes of sufficient force and validity to bind the colonies and people of America, subjects of the crown of Great Britain, in all cases whatsoever."

In 1774, Warren was elected as a representative to the Massachusetts Provincial Congress. The Massachusetts House of Representatives had elected delegates to send to Philadelphia for the First Continental Congress. Thomas Gage arrived in May to replace Thomas Hutchinson as Governor General and was welcomed at a reception in Faneuil Hall. Gage soon announced the Boston Port Bill, which closed the port of Boston until the East India Company was compensated 9,000 pounds sterling for the tea destroyed by the Tea Party; and the colony was required to agree to the Townshend duty on tea.

A town meeting at Faneuil Hall on May 13th resolved that the Committee of Correspondence circulate a letter throughout all the other colonies asking for an intercolonial boycott of British goods. As chairman of the Committee of Correspondence, Dr. Warren is credited with writing the *Solemn League and Covenant*, soliciting each town to support the boycott and encourage each citizen to publicly swear to such a pledge. Joseph Warren was also made chairman of a new standing Committee of Donations, to accept donations from throughout the colonies.

In late August 1774, Dr. Warren wrote the patriotic words:

When liberty is the prize, who would shun the warfare? Who would stoop to waste a coward thought on life? We esteem no sacrifice too great, no conflict too severe, to redeem our inestimable rights and privileges. 'Tis for you, brethren, for ourselves, for our united posterity, we hazard all; and permit us humbly to hope, that such a measure of vigilance, fortitude, and perseverance will still be afforded us, that, by patiently suffering and nobly daring, we may eventually secure that more precious than Hesperian" fruit, the golden apples of freedom. We eye the hand of Heaven in the rapid and wonderful union of the colonies; and that generous and universal emulation to prevent the sufferings of the people of this place gives a prelibation of the cup of deliverance. May unerring Wisdom dictate the measures to be recommended by the [Continental] Congress! May a smiling God conduct this people through the thorny paths of difficulty, and finally gladden our hearts with success![48]

Native Bostonian Thomas Hutchinson (1711-1780) served Massachusetts well in the mid-1700s as speaker of the colonial assembly and lieutenant governor, but as the 1760s progressed, his loyalties to the crown put him in conflict with the growing patriotic fervor. The last colonial governor of Massachusetts, he left for England in 1774 to consult with the king and never returned.

Warren wrote on another occasion,

Our enemies, we know, will use every artifice that hell can suggest and human power can execute to enslave us; but we are determined not to submit. We choose to effect our salvation from bondage by policy, rather than by arms; considering that the blood of freemen who fight for their country is of more value than the blood of a soldiery who fight for pay."[49]

Dr. Warren wrote the Suffolk County Resolves declaring themselves to be free of recent British acts, the unfair Provincial courts and justice system, and the imposed taxation apparatus. He stated that "...it is an indispensable duty which we owe to God, our country, ourselves, and posterity, by all lawful ways and means in our power, to maintain, defend, and preserve those civil and religious rights and liberties for which many of our fathers fought, bled, and died, and to hand them down entire to future generations."

On September 9, scores of patriots representing nineteen districts and towns were assembled in Milton, Massachusetts, where Warren read the Suffolk Resolves aloud to the cheers and approbation of the delegates, who voted unanimously in favor. Two biographers, John Cary and Richard Frothingham, among others, concluded that Warren was the author and that it was his most important and influential piece of writing. Although the document professed loyalty to the king, it was an insurrectionary document. It instructed colonists to reject the acts of Parliament and to prepare to defend themselves against the violent onslaught that Britain would likely unleash because of their disobedience. In the Resolves, Warren noted that Boston's streets were "...thronged with military executioners..." and its "...harbors crowded with ships of war...." Citing the "...unrelenting severity of Britain's use of power..." and the "...gross infractions of those rights to which we [the colonists] are justly entitled...", he concluded that the " ....encroachment of [our] liberty..." was omnipresent. On September 16, Paul Revere arrived in Philadelphia with the Suffolk Resolves. The following day, the document was presented to the Continental Congress whose members applauded as it was read aloud. The resolutions were approved and adopted unanimously. John Adams recorded in his diary that day, "This was one of the happiest days of my life.... This day convinced me that America will support Massachusetts or perish with her."[50]

On Monday, March 6, 1775, Warren authored an article that appeared in the *Boston Evening Post*, in which he argued that "...the Americans would be compelled by the great law of nature to strike a decisive blow; and publish a manifesto to the world showing the necessity of dissolving their connection with a nation whose ministers were aiming at their ruin." A little over a year later, Thomas Jefferson would echo Warren's thoughts by using his words in the Declaration of Independence — the "great law of nature" and "the necessity of dissolving their connection."[51]

The First Massachusetts Provincial Congress convened at Salem on October 7, 1774 (dissolved on December 10) with Dr. Warren as a delegate.[52] Among the 290 delegates sent by Massachusetts towns included the often mentioned names of Boston's Sons of Liberty: John Hancock, Dr. Joseph Warren, Thomas Cushing, Samuel Adams, Dr. Benjamin Church, and Nathaniel Appleton. Warren was chairman of the Committee of Correspondence, Committee of Safety[53], Committee of Donations, Committee of Supplies, the North End Caucus, and in 1775, was President pro rem (later President) of the Massachusetts Provincial Congress. Each year, Warren was asked to give the memorial address honoring those killed in the Boston Massacre of March 5, 1770.[54] He was the best orator and most eloquent speaker among Boston's Sons of Liberty. His entry into politics was prompted by his strong patriotic desire for liberty and freedom and his simultaneous opposition to taxation without representation. Writing under the pseudonym "B.W." to the *Boston Gazette* on Oct. 7, 1765, he stated,

> ...Awake, my countrymen, and by a regular and legal opposition, defeat the designs of those who would enslave us and our posterity. Nothing is wanting, but your own resolu-

Paul Revere titled his engraving of the 1770 altercation in Boston between British troops and local belligerents "The Bloody Massacre." History calls it the Boston Massacre. Through his engravings, Revere documented a number of the historic moments in his hometown that led up to the Revolution.

The Boston Gazette *ran this drawing of the coffins of four of the Americans who died in the Boston Massacre, with their initials on top. The fourth, Crispus Attucks, was a man of Native American and African descent. All four, along with a fifth casualty, were buried together in Boston's Granary Burying Yard.*

tion — For great is the authority, exalted the dignity, and powerful the majesty of the People.... Ages remote, mortals yet unborn, will bless your generous efforts, and revere the memory of the saviours of their country.... By the unconquerable spirit of the ancient Britons; — by the genious of that constitution which abhors every species of vassallage; — by the august title of Englishman; — by the grand prerogatives of human nature; the lovely image of the Infinite Deity — and what is more than all, by the liberty wherewith Christ has made you free; I exhort you to instruct your representatives against promoting by any ways or means whatsoever, the operation of this grevious and burdensome law.[55]

The Stamp Act was repealed on March 18, 1766, but was replaced by an even worse Declaratory Act.

As the antagonism between the colonies and Great Britain grew, a corresponding, unintended undercurrent of agitation automatically developed. Joseph Warren's precocious intellect, eloquent speech, affable manners, handsome features, and thorough knowledge and skill in his profession quickly rendered him a general favorite, allowing for his rapid success as an eminent and esteemed physician. Since he treated every patient impartially — Whig and Tory, rich and poor, enemy and friend, young and old — he became everyone's favorite, so his practice quickly developed into the largest and most acclaimed in Boston. In that enviable position, he acquired information from the entire spectrum of both British and colonial political thought. Indeed, his office became an espionage center where patriot spies from all levels of society filtered their vital intelligence. Dr. Warren's American nationalism and patriotism developed steadily as the chasm widened and the gulf deepened between colonial and British social, political, and military interests.

Elizabeth Hooton Warren died May 23, 1773, within a few days of the death of Paul Revere's first wife. Both women probably succumbed to an infectious disease circulating that spring. She was twenty-six years old and the mother of four young children. She assured Joseph, as well as her parson that she was prepared to die. She expressed her love and concern for Joseph and the children. Her final requests were that her wedding band be given to Betsey (Elizabeth, the oldest child) and that she be buried alongside little Mary (a daughter who died in infancy; their next child, a daughter, was also named Mary).[56]

The Emblem of the Effects of the Stamp appeared in the Pennsylvania Journal in 1765 as a protest against the hated Stamp Act.

The famous "Join, or Die" snake remains the first known American cartoon. Published in 1754 by Benjamin Franklin in the Pennsylvania Gazette, it admonishes the colonists to support his plan for union, presented at the Albany Congress.

Dr. Warren, grief-stricken after having laid his "dearest friend" to rest, wrote a poem in her honor, which appeared in the *Boston Gazette* along with her obituary:

If fading Lilies, when they droop and die
Rob'd of each charm that pleas'd the gazing
    Eye,
With sad Regret the grieving Mind inspire,
What then when Virtue's brightest Lamps
    expire?

Premature deaths were a grim reality facing colonists in a period fraught with disease, epidemics, folk remedies, and lack of modern medicines. Warren, now thirty-one and a

Contemporary sketch of Warren's mourning ring for his deceased wife, Elizabeth Hooten Warren, based on a sketch and description of the ring from Providence Evening Press, June 14, 1875. Illustration by Mark Stutzman.

Joseph Warren's home, nineteenth century engraving. Warren rented this house on Hanover Street in the North End, where he lived from 1772 with his family and apprentices and conducted his medical practice. Warren triggered the Lexington Alarm and the beginning of the Revolutionary War from his office here, as he dispatched Paul Revere and William Dawes on their missions to warn the Patriot militia of British army movements on the evening of April 18, 1775. (Courtesy of the Bostonian Society)

widower with four young children, had little time to grieve, let alone search for a new love. He was attempting to run one of the busiest medical practices in Boston while spearheading the colony's fight against British oppression.

On April 18, 1775, after seeing his last patient at his office/home on Hanover Street, Dr. Warren heard a faint rapping at the door. When he opened the door, a hooded figure quickly stepped inside and asked, "Are we alone?" After being assured of their privacy, a lady removed the hooded cloak and revealed herself as Margaret Kemble Gage, the wife of Governor General Thomas Gage. Both she and her husband were (or had been) patients of Dr. Warren. In his office records, he listed her as "Camp Woman" in order to avoid any questions should his records ever be examined. She began, "You told me once that I could count on you. If I should learn of some critical design, you would discreetly place the fact into the faction's camp, in order to avoid a disaster to our distressed country. I fear that time is now. The army bestirs. Your misguided compatriots have been organizing for a fight. Let my husband's army pass to their object without incident. Stop this madness if you possibly can." He responded, "Tell me exactly what is afoot. What is the troops' object?" Mrs. Gage hesitated, "They speak of reclaiming the King's stores." Warren pressed her, "Where? Have they named a place?"

"Surely you must know that they, and you for that matter, can be arrested [for treason] at any time. They speak of Concord town. Weapons gathering there belong to [the] Government. Muskets, powder, fearsome cannons in the rabble hands! Your [John] Hancock and [Samuel] Adams sulking nearby for the plucking." Warren nodded, "I can promise you this, Mrs. Gage, the country people will endeavor to face the soldiery for Constitutional and their Charter Rights and for posterity's sake, but they will not fire unless fired upon. If blood be spilt, it will not be our doing." Mrs. Gage paused and then voiced her immediate concern, "There must be no word of my ever being here." "Yes, Madam. Do not fear. I will take your secret to the grave." She quickly replaced her hooded cloak, peeked out from behind the drapes to be sure no one was nearby, and hastily exited the office door.[57]

Dr. Warren quickly summoned Paul Revere and William Dawes, a local tanner, to his office to inform them. Dawes was to go into the countryside overland by way of the neck, while Revere was to go inland by way of Charlestown ferry, the same route Dr. Warren would take later that evening. Their largest arsenal was at Concord, and John Hancock and Samuel Adams were staying at Rev. Jonas Clark's house in Lexington, near the road to Concord. The Committee of Safety was meeting that evening at the Black Horse Tavern in Menotom[e]y (now Arlington), also along the route to Concord."

As British troops lumbered out of Boston in the chill night of April 18, Paul Revere and William Dawes galloped ahead of them, spreading the warning that the redcoats were coming. The British met with unexpected local opposition through the following day, until they were joined by reinforcements under Lord Perry.

As extravagant as his famous signature, Hancock reigned as one of the wealthiest men in New England, yet he was a lifelong populist. By the late 1760s, he and Samuel Adams had become leading figures in the Sons of Liberty, and at the Second Continental Congress Hancock served as president and the first signer of the Declaration of Independence. With war on the horizon, he hoped he would be made commander in chief of the Conti-

Mrs. Gage, by John Singleton Copley, 1771. Margaret Kemble Gage, with close friends on both sides, is suspected by some as Warren's source of military intelligence about her husband's foray to Lexington and Concord. Courtesy of the Putnam Foundation, Timken Museum of Art, San Diego, California.

Thomas Gage, by John Singleton Copley. An experienced officer and head of British military forces in North America, Gage was appointed as governor general in Massachusetts following the Destruction of the Tea. Warren interacted through intermediaries with his opponent Gage during the early months of the Siege of Boston. (Courtesy of the Yale Center for British Art, Paul Mellon Collection)

Boston's Old North (Christ) Church earned a place in history on the night of April 18, 1775, when two sextons hung lanterns from its steeple in a prearranged signal to Paul Revere about British troop movements. Poet Henry Wadsworth Longfellow later immortalized the signal as "One if by land, and two if by sea" in his classic, Paul Revere's Ride.

nental forces. When that position went to George Washington, Hancock continued as president of the congress for another year, then as a delegate and active supporter of the Revolution, helping to secure supplies and troops for the army. In 1780 he was elected the first governor of Massachusetts, and in the first presidential election his name was entered as one of the candidates. Once again, Washington was chosen over him, yet throughout the early formation of America, the two men complemented and supported each other in the cause of liberty.

Later that evening, Warren met with patriot General William Heath at the meeting of the Committee of Safety. At Lexington and Concord, he followed Heath into battle, both treating the wounded as well as engaging in the particularly intense fighting in which he was nearly killed. A musket ball came so close to him "…as to take off a lock of his hair which curled close to his head."[59] He also fought at Grape

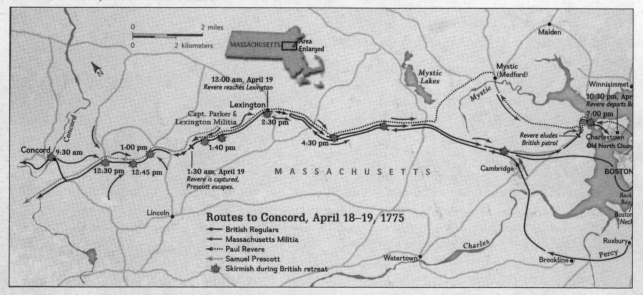

Routes to Concord, April 18–19, 1775

- ← British Regulars
- ← Massachusetts Militia
- ← Paul Revere
- ← Samuel Prescott
- ✳ Skirmish during British retreat

Paul Revere, by John Singleton Copley, 1768. The silversmith, Patriot Express rider, and jack of many trades met and befriended Joseph Warren in the St. Andrew's Lodge of Masons, where both held leadership positions. (Museum of Fine Arts, Boston. Gift of Joseph Revere, William B. Revere, and Edward H.R. Revere. Photograph © 2010 Museum of Fine Arts, Boston.

John Hancock, 1737–1793

Island and in the Battle of Noddle's Island. The period between Lexington and Concord and the Battle of Bunker Hill (Breed's Hill) has been referred to as the "sixty days". Warren was the only patriot leader — both civilian and military — who personally engaged in all four skirmishes and battles within this time frame. He advanced the rebellion into a revolution by organizing a provincial army with militia from Massachusetts, New Hampshire, Connecticut, and Rhode Island.

When Dr. Warren left his home/office to meet Paul Revere at Lexington/Concord, he was never able to return. Knowing that his life was increasingly in peril, in February, he arranged through his friend and colleague, Dr. Elijah Dix, to purchase a house and twenty acres of land in Worcester. Dr. Dix arranged for Dr. Warren's possessions from Boston and Roxbury to be transported to Worcester. Dr. Dix was also asked to see that Mercy Scollay (Warren's wife-to-be) and his children were safely cared for. Any of his possessions that could not be quickly moved were taken to Mercy Scollay's parents' home for safekeeping. Just prior to the Battles of Lexington and Concord, Dr. Warren "... said his goodbyes to Mercy and his four children as he loaded them into his carriage, then watched as they rode off toward Worcester. It was the last time he would ever see them."[60]

The British troops retreating from Lexington and Concord reached Charlestown around sunset. One British soldier wrote, "They fought like bears, and I would as soon storm hell as fight them." That day, the British forces suffered nearly three hundred casualties, about three times the number of American casualties.

On the afternoon of Wednesday, June 14, the Third Provincial Congress made Joseph Warren, M.D. a major general. That same day, the Second Continental Congress in Philadelphia established the Continental Army for the common defense of the colonies. The next day, Col. George Washington of Virginia was appointed its commanding general with General Artemas Ward second-in-command.

The Committee of Safety received intelligence "...of undoubted veracity..." that Gage intended to take Bunker Hill and Dorchester Heights on June 18th. It was decided by the Provincial Congress in Watertown on June 15 that the colonial forces would defend the highest point on the Charlestown peninsula, i.e. Bunker Hill. Gen. Israel Putnam and Col. William Prescott, along with chief engineer and head of artillery Col. Richard Gridey, reconnoitered.

They ultimately decided to fortify Breed's Hill rather than Bunker Hill. Breed's Hill was more vulnerable to attack, especially to cannon fire from ships docked on the Charles River, but the colonial command could better monitor activities in Boston and the approaching British forces. Under the cover of darkness on June 16, they hurriedly worked through the night, digging trenches and constructing earthen walls, since at daybreak they realized that the British command would discover these new fortifications and quickly attack.

As soon as Dr. Warren heard that the attack had begun, he rushed to the redoubt at the crest of Breed's Hill, which was the command center. Several friends and colleagues attempted to dissuade him from joining the battle. General Putnam and Col. Prescott offered the command to Major General Warren; but since his commission had not yet officially arrived, and since the troops had no knowledge of his new rank, he declined the offer. Instead, he took his place in the trenches as a regular infantry soldier. Armed with a pistol, sword,

Whatever skills Harvard-educated Samuel Adams lacked as a businessman and Boston maltster, he made up for as a political agitator. In 1747, while still in his mid-20s, the puritanical Adams was elected to his first public office. By the time the British imposed the Stamp Act in 1765, he was well positioned to foment local opposition against it. As a delegate to the Massachusetts House, he continued his protest of new taxes and duties and later of the British occupation of Boston. In the days preceding the Revolution, Adams moved from agitation to action, and he is often credited with playing a leading part in organizing the Boston Tea Party, although historians disagree about his actual role. As a delegate to the First and Second Continental Congresses he signed the Declaration of Independence and helped draft the Articles of Confederation. In 1781 he left Congress and returned to Boston, where he continued to agitate for public virtue in politics.

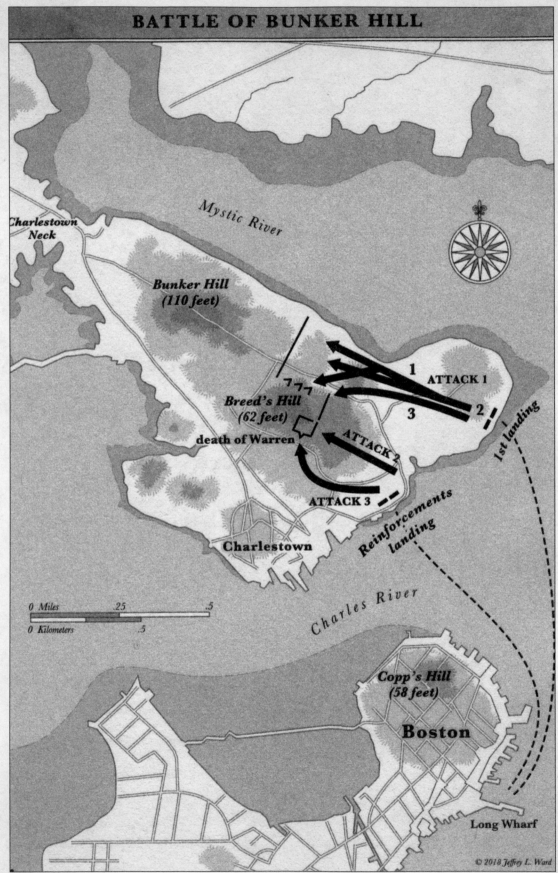

BATTLE OF BUNKER HILL

Charlestown Neck

Mystic River

Bunker Hill (110 feet)

Breed's Hill (62 feet)

death of Warren

ATTACK 1

1

2

3

1st landing

ATTACK 2

ATTACK 3

Reinforcements landing

Charlestown

Charles River

0 Miles   .25   .5

0 Kilometers   .5

Copp's Hill (58 feet)

Boston

Long Wharf

© 2018 Jeffrey L. Ward

Troop fortifications and movements during the Battle of Bunker Hill.

and musket and his cherished Bible, which he always carried in his pocket, he entered the fighting. After repulsing the British charge three times, the colonial forces were compelled to retreat after their ammunition was expended. Maj. Gen. Warren was one of the last to leave the entrenchments, allowing the troops to evacuate first. His arm bleeding from a bayonet thrust, he had proceeded only a few steps when a "...British officer seized a musket and shot him in the skull behind the ear."[61]

Warren had voluntarily sacrificed himself to protect his men, giving his life for the patriot cause. The following morning, Sunday, June 18th, British troops returned to the battlefield to bury their dead. When word of Warren's death reached the British command, they refused to believe that the top Whig commander, in charge of the major political, social, and military bodies in Massachusetts, would have risked his life by personally fighting. British troops vented their fury upon him, stripped off his clothing, looted his personal items including his cherished Bible, his sword, pistols, and letters, and papers he had tucked in the fold of his waistcoat." His Majesty's soldiers repeatedly bayoneted his corpse, "...violently butchering ..." him. "Lt. James Drew of the Royal Navy returned to the redoubt, walked over to Warren's body, and spat in his face before cutting off his head. He was hastily buried in a trench, his mutilated corpse tossed unceremoniously into a shallow ditch...,"[63] and "...stuffed the scoundrel with another into one hole and there he and his seditious principles may remain."[64] He died as he earlier wished, "knee deep in blood." It took three full days to completely remove the wounded and bury the dead.

Abigail Adams wrote to her husband, John, in Philadelphia where he was a Massachusetts delegate to the Second Continental Congress,

> I have just heard that our dear friend, Dr. Warren is no more, but fell gloriously fighting for his country, saying better to die honorably in the war than ignominiously hang upon the gallows. Great is our loss! Not all the havoc and devastation they [the British] have made has wounded me like the death of Warren. We want him in the Senate, we want him in his profession, we want him in the field. We mourn for the citizen, the senator, the physician and the warrior. When he fell, liberty wept.

John Adams replied, "Our dear Warren, has fallen, with Laurells on his Brow, as fresh and blooming, as ever graced an Hero."

A fellow member of the Massachusetts Committee of Safety with Warren, when reporting through the Massachusetts delegation to the Continental Congress, bestowed the hero's label on Warren:

> Our good, our beloved friend Dr. Warren was on Bunker Hill [Breed's Hill] when the lines were forced and is no more, he was two days before chosen Major General. Accepted on Friday and on Saturday died like a hero. We can only drop a tear for our worthy brother and console ourselves with the consideration that his virtue and valour will be rewarded in heaven."[65]

The Death of General Warren at the Battle of Bunker Hill, June 17, 1775, by John Trumbull, 1786–87. This painting shows the death of Gen. Joseph Warren at the Battle of Bunker Hill. A Boston physician and leader of the patriots, Warren dispatched Paul Revere on his midnight ride and harassed the British line as it marched from Concord to Boston. His death became a rallying point for the colonial cause.

Abigail Smith Adams, pastel by Blythe, 1760s. Like her husband, Abigail Adams also became Warren's patient and friend. She probably looked on anxiously as Warren treated the seriously injured finger of her son, future president John Quincy Adams. (Courtesy of the Massachusetts Historical Society)

Abigail Smith Adams, 1744–1818
Born on November 11, 1744, Abigail Smith grew up in Weymouth, Massachusetts. Her father was the pastor of the local church, and young Abigail took advantage of her father's well-stocked library, studying the Bible, history, philosophy, and poetry. Her future husband, lawyer John Adams, found her erudition attractive, and the two were married in 1764. Their marriage was a strong one, enduring the long absences that resulted from her husband's career. Abigail wrote often to her husband, and her political legacy can be found in many of these letters. An advocate for women's rights and education, Adams believed that women should be recognized for their intellectual capabilities and as much more than mere companions for their husbands. While John Adams was at the Continental Congress in 1776, she famously wrote to them to "remember the ladies, and be more generous and favorable to them than your ancestors… Remember all Men would be tyrants if they could."

In late May, Dr. Warren had written:

> "I know the temper of our people. They are sensible, brave, and virtuous; and I wish they might ever continue so. Mild and gentle regulations will be sufficient for them; but the penalties annexed to the breach of those rules should be rigorously inflicted. I would have such a government as should give every man the greatest freedom to do what he pleases consistent with restraining him from doing any injury to another, or such a government as would most contribute to the good of the whole, with the least inconvenience to individuals."

He continued,

> "The sword should, in all free States, be subservient to the civil powers...."[66]

Warren pledged himself shortly before his death, "To the persecution and tyranny of the cruel ministry, we will not tamely submit — appealing to heaven for the justice of our cause, we determine to die or to be free." Earlier he had admonished all who would follow: "On you depend the fortunes of America. You are to decide the important question, on which rests the happiness and liberty of millions yet unborn. Act worthy of yourselves."

Innumerable eulogies were written about Dr. Warren's death. The following represent the last three quatrains of Miss Mercy Scollay's 21-quatrain poem about Dr. Joseph Warren, her fiancé[67]:

O'Warren! Could thy Country's Pray'rs prevail,
And call thy Spirit from its Kindred Skies,
In vain bright Cherubs might the loss bewail,
Contending Mortals would unseal thine Eyes!

But shall weak Man presume thus to repine
And murmur at th' Almighty's high Degree.
Or wish to check th' unerring Hand Devine,
Which snatch'd Thee hence to Immortality?

No, Rather let thy Great Example fire
Each gen'rous Great to emulate the fame.
And so thy Vast, Unbounded Height aspire
To catch a spark from thy Celestial Flame.[68]

"The last best chapter of Joseph Warren's life was, to be sure, his finest. Born the son of a Roxbury farmer, he had peddled milk [and apples] to the Boston market as a barelegged boy. By the age of thirty-four, he was widely known as a competent physician, a skillful politician, and a sincere patriot. As a physician he stood at the top of his profession in Boston, and did much to train [he had numerous apprentices] the next generation of doctors in Massachusetts, the men who served as army surgeons during the war. In politics, Warren ranked with Samuel Adams as one of two most important men in forming a political party that influenced colony politics for twenty years. Without assuming public office until 1775, he led the Bay Colony in forcing the recall of Frances Bernard [Governor General], in fighting for local control of offices and policies, in gaining repeal of parliamentary taxes, and in driving British troops from Boston. Through press, orations, instruction, caucus, committees, and town meetings, he expressed the growing sentiment against the domination of Massachusetts politics by a pro-British party. But Warren was much more than a publicist for the revolutionary cause; he was also an able organizer and director of his political party and of the political activities of such groups as the masonic lodges and the North End artisans. He was a key figure in the *Liberty* incident, the [Boston] Massacre trial, the formation of the Committee of Correspondence, the Committee of Safety, and the Boston Tea Party. Warren was perhaps the most important man in creating the Provincial Congress; he fought to give Massachusetts a completely democratic government and, in his Suffolk Resolves, he sounded the keynote for some of the most important policies adopted by the Continental Congress.... Joseph Warren's leadership was effective because he believed in the same things as did the people of Massachusetts. He expressed in his life the nationalism, the desire for home rule, and the demand for a government responsive to the electorate that were becoming articles of a new American faith."

"While Warren's mortal road ended on Bunker Hill [Breed's Hill], to the extent we remain true to the best of the founders' legacies, our path continues assuredly in aspiration of American liberty."[69] Dr. Warren was in fact, both the symbolic and the literal executive of the revolutionary government. Warren prophesied and correctly predicted, "I am of [the] opinion that, if once General [Thomas] Gage should lead his troops into the country with designs to enforce the last acts of Parliament, Great Britain may take her leave, at least of the New England colonies, and if I mistake not, of all America."

Daniel Webster called Dr. Joseph Warren, "...the first great martyr in the great cause." Lewis Collins said of Warren, "He had the qualities of a great leader and had his life been spared to the close of the war he would probably have ranked next to Washington among the great generals of that war." Others have predicted that had he lived, he would have been Washington's military equal, if not superior, and would have been the first President of the United States with Mercy Scollay [Warren] as his, and our, First Lady.

Major General Joseph Warren, M.D. was intellectually precocious, a brilliant student, astute politician, brave soldier, dedicated revolutionary, distinguished patriot, faithful nationalist, elegant orator, talented writer, outstanding leader, eminent and acclaimed physician, loving husband, caring father, devout Christian, and courageous defender of freedom, possessing handsome features and affable manners. He never sought power or fame, yet he became the most powerful leader in the revolutionary cause and the best known and most popular of all colonial leaders. "The name of Warren will be enrolled at the head of that band of patriots and heroes, who sacrificed their lives to purchase the independence of America."[71] Alexander Everett wrote, "To Warren, distinguished as he was among the bravest, wisest, and best of the patriotic band, was assigned, in the inscrutable decrees of Providence, the crown of early martyrdom.... The blood of martyrs has been, in all ages, the nourishing rain of religion and liberty" *(Life of Joseph Warren)*. "The tears of multitudes pay tribute to his memory" (Abigail Adams, June 18, 1775). "He closed a life of glory in a glorious death; and heaven never received the spirit of a purer patriot" (Abigail Adams, July 5, 1775).

Warren County could not have been named for anyone nobler or more deserving of the honor.

Jerry W. Martin, M.D.

"Our country is in danger....Our streets are again filled with armed men. Our harbor is crowded with ships of war. But these cannot intimidate us.... Our liberty must be preserved. It is far dearer than life.... On you depend the fortunes of America. You are to decide the important question, on which rests the happiness and liberty of millions yet unborn. Act worthy of yourselves."*

Joseph Warren, M.D.'s speech commemorating the 1770 Boston Massacre
Monday, March 6, 1775
Old South Meeting House
Milk and Washington Streets
Boston, Massachusetts

The British Are Coming, The War for America, pp. 36-38, Rick Atkinson.

FREE AMERICA

We led fair freedom hither
And lo, the desert smiled
A paradise of pleasure
Was opened in the wild!
Your harvest bold Americans
No power shall snatch away
Huzza, huzza, huzza, huzza
    For free America!

Torn from a world of tyrants
Beneath his western sky
We formed a new dominion
A land of liberty
The world shall own we're masters here
Then hasten on the day
Oppose, oppose, oppose, oppose
    For free America!

Lift up your hands, ye heroes
And swear with proud disdain
The Wretch that would ensnare you
Shall lay his snares in vain;
Should Europe empty all her force,
We'll meet her in array,
And fight and shout, and shout and fight
    For North America!

Some future day shall crown us
The masters of the main
Our fleets shall speak of Thunder
To England, France, and Spain
And the nations over the oceans spread
I Shall tremble and obey
The sons, the sons, the sons, the sons
    Of brave America!

—By Dr. Joseph Warren, 1774

Published in colonial newspapers, the poem was set to a traditional British tune, "The British Grenadiers". (Jerry Silverman, "Of Thee I Sing", Citadel Press, 2002, p.3.)

ENDNOTES

1   Joseph Warren's words to Samuel Adams, June 15, 1774.
2   The words were attributed to Joseph Warren [III] by Elbridge Gerry who said that Warren uttered the remark during the days just prior to the Battle of Breed's Hill. The Latin quote by Warren is from the Roman poet Horace's (Quintus Horatius Flaccus, 65-8 B.C.) *Odes* III, verse 2, line 13: "It is a sweet and proper thing to die for one's country."
3   *Life of Joseph Warren*, Alexander H. Everett, L.L.D.
4   *Founding Martyr; The Life and Death of Dr. Joseph Warren, the American Revolution's Lost Hero*, Christian Di Spigna, 2018.
5   *Life and Times of Joseph Warren*, Richard Frothingham, 1865.
6   Op. cit., Alexander Everett.
7   *Genealogy of Warren, With Some Historical Sketches*, printed in 1854. An account of the Warren surname was listed in the *Patronymica Britannica* dated October 1, 1860.
8   Op. cit., Richard Frothingham.
9   *Dr. Joseph Warren: The Boston Tea Party, Bunker Hill, and The Birth of American Liberty*, Samuel A. Forman, M.D.
10   Peter Warren (1631-1704). One year after his birth, the *Arbella* brought settlers to North America to form the Massachusetts Bay Colony.
11   Suffolk County records list Peter Warren as a mariner.
12   Before the mid-twentieth century, many women died of puerperal fever ("childbirth fever"). Sulfa drugs were not developed until the mid- to late 1930s, and then penicillin, in the early 1940s. The infection was endometritis (infection of the lining of the uterus). (Puerperal: pyu er per al, L.*puer*, child; *pario*, to bring forth.)
13   Deborah Williams was a sister of Rev. John Williams who was a captive of the French Canadian Indians in the Deerfield raid of 1704. John Demos related the event in his book, *The Unredeemed Captive*.
14   Presumably Esther had died.
15   Mary Stevens' father was Samuel Stevens, M.D. of Roxbury, Massachusetts.
16   John Warren, M.D., was twelve years younger than Joseph, but he also served as a physician/surgeon in the war.
17   The house on Braintree Road at the farm in Roxbury still stands.
18   Russet apples were referred to locally as "Warren russets" or "Roxbury russets".
19   *Boston Gazette*, October 27, 1755; *Boston Evening Post*, October 27. He was buried in the Old Burying Ground, known to the elders as the Eliot Burying Ground (named for Rev. John Eliot). The cost of the funeral was forty pounds, which was equivalent to approximately 800 days' pay for a laborer and only slightly less than Joseph Warren earned teaching for a year at Roxbury Latin School after graduating from Harvard.
20   Op. cit., Christian Di Spigna.
21   Ibid.
22   Usually listed as Battle of Bunker Hill, June 17, 1775.

23 Ibid., Christian Di Spigna.

24 Joseph began Roxbury Latin School at age 10.

25 Contemporary figures are examples: John Adams (Harvard) did postgraduate teaching in Milton, Massachusetts; and Nathan Hale (Yale) taught in New London, Connecticut.

26 Op. cit., Samuel A. Forman.

27 Cato committed suicide rather than submit to tyranny as Caesar's victory loomed. Joseph Addison (1612-1719), English essayist and poet.

28 Ibid., Samuel A. Forman.

29 Dr. Hermann Boerhaave, a Dutch physician (1669-1738). Warren challenged the long held humeral theory of disease.

30 Op. cit., Christian Di Spigna.

31 Joseph had graduated from Harvard at age 18 and completed his two-year apprenticeship in 1763. He also had taught at the Roxbury Latin School, as well as prepared his Masters dissertation.

32 Ibid., Christian Di Spigna.

33 Op. cit., Samuel A. Forman.

34 Ibid., Samuel A. Forman.

35 Op. cit., Janet Uhlar. Josiah Quincy was an attorney and second cousin of John Quincy Adams. He was a Massachusetts state legislator, member of the U.S. House of Representatives, mayor of Boston and president of Harvard College.

36 Ibid., Janet Uhlar, p. 87.

37 Op. cit., Christian Di Spigna.

38 *Boston Gazette*, September 10, 1764; *Boston Post Boy*, September 10, 1764.

39 *Boston Evening Post*, June 4, 1764.

40 Op. cit., Samuel A. Forman.

41 Joseph had moved from Roxbury to Boston to establish a practice there.

42 Peter Oliver (Loyalist, Tory) said of Cooper that "...no man could, with a better grace, utter the word of God from his mouth and at the same time keep a two edged dagger concealed in his hand and mix privately, with the rabble, in their mightly seditious associations."

43 Op. cit., Christian Di Spigna.

44 Ibid., Christian Di Spigna. Anglo-French contentions over North America triggered the Seven Years' War. In 1754, Virginia dispatched an army under Lt. Colonel George Washington to construct a fort at the head of the Ohio River (present-day Pittsburgh, Pennsylvania). A French force was moving southward to accomplish the same goal. When these forces made contact, Washington ordered an attack, resulting in the death of ten French soldiers. Several colonies raised armies to assist in the territories west of the Appalachian Mountains and in Champlain Valley in the north. By 1755, Britain had succeeded in only controlling Nova Scotia. They confiscated French property and moved over 6,000 Acadians from their homes and relocated them throughout the colonies, especially to Louisiana (their descendants are called Cajuns). Early in 1756, Britain and France finally declared war. The English colonists called the conflict the

French War, but historians have referred to it variously as the Seven Years' War and the French and Indian War, as well as the Great War for the Empire. The hostilities in the north ended, but the conflict raged in the south against Cherokee Indians until 1761. In the Treaty of Paris of 1763, France ceded to England the territory east of the Mississippi River, south of the Ohio River and west of the Appalachian Mountains, except for the Isle d'Orleans. After the French threat ended, differences between London and the American colonies quickly surfaced into open conflict over westward expansion, Indian relations, taxation without representation, authority, power, and ultimate control.

45   Ibid., Christian Di Spigna.

46   The letter is Warren's earliest surviving personal letter.

47   Hesperides (N. pl., Hesperid, sing. Gr. myth.): the nymphs who guarded the golden apples given as a wedding gift by Gaea [Gr. Gaia, earth]. The earth personified as a goddess, Hera, the wife of Zeus, queen of the gods and goddess of marriage; identified with the Roman goddess Juno.

48   Joseph Warren to the Stonington Committee, August 24, 1774.

49   Joseph Warren to the Preston Committee, August 24, 1774.

50   Op. cit., Christian Di Spigna.

51   The Suffolk County Convention, called in lieu of the proscribed town meetings in Massachusetts, adopted the resolutions introduced by Joseph Warren, M.D. on September 9, 1774. These resolutions declared that no obedience ought to be paid to the Coercive Acts; that taxes ought to be collected by the Provincial Congress and withheld from the royal government until the government of Massachusetts had been "...placed upon a constitutional foundation..."; that military preparations ought to be made against the danger of attack by the British troops in Boston; and that, if a patriot leader was seized by the British, the citizens were justified in imprisoning "...every servant of the present tyrannical and unconstitutional government." *Origins of the American Revolution*, John C. Miller.

52   This was Joseph Warren's first popularly elected office.

53   The Committee of Safety was the ruling body of the colony when the Provincial Congress was not in session.

54   On March 5, 1770, a patriot mob harassed a contingent of British soldiers on guard duty outside the State House in Boston. The troops fired, killing three immediately; two more died within days; and others were shot, but survived.

55   *Boston Gazette*, October 7, 1765.

56   Op. cit., Richard Frothingham; and *Joseph Warren: Physician, Politician, Patriot*, John Cary. Warren's four living children were committed to the care of their grandmothers, Mrs. Richard Hooton and Mrs. Joseph Warren (II). Their names were Elizabeth ("Betsey"), Joseph ("Josey"), Mary ("Polly"), and Richard ("Dickey"). They also periodically lived with Joseph's mother and his brother, John Warren, M.D. and his family, and later with Miss Mercy Scollay, the woman Joseph was engaged to at the time of his death.

57   Op. cit., Christian Di Spigna.

58 Op. cit., Samuel A. Forman. Who can forget the times we have read Henry Wadsworth Longfellow's (1807-1882) "Paul Revere's Ride" or Ralph Waldo Emerson's (1803-1882) "Concord Hymn".

59 Op. cit., Christian Di Spigna.

60 Ibid., Christian Di Spigna.

61 Op. cit, Samuel A. Forman. This is apparently untrue. On August 3, 1855, John Collins Warren, M.D. (Joseph's brother John's son) observed while removing the remains of Joseph Warren from the vault in St. Paul Cathedral, "The hole created by the ball that struck General Warren in the face was clearly visible, as was the larger orifice [exit wound] to the rear of his head." Viewing the two pictures of Dr. Warren's skull, the lethal ball (smaller caliber than a musket ball) struck him in the left cheek below the eye, penetrated the maxillary sinus, traversed through the midbrain and basal ganglia, and exited the contralateral occipital area (right posterior base of the skull). There are numerous other versions of his shooting, usually listing the Weapon as a musket; however, the weapon had to have been a pistol because of the size of the entrance wound.

62 Op. cit., Christian Di Spigna.

63 Op. cit., Samuel A. Forman. Legend has it that Warren's body was identified by John Jefferson. Lt. Walter Laurie was in charge of the detail to bury the dead.

64 Op. cit., Christian Di Spigna.

65 Elbridge Gerry to the Massachusetts delegates at the Continental Congress, June 30, 1775.

66 Op. cit., Samuel A. Forman.

67 Dr. Dix, April 1776. Mercy Scollay's Papers.

68 Op. cit., John Cary.

69 Op. cit., Samuel A. Forman

70 *History of Kentucky*, Lewis Collins.

71 *History of the Rise, Progress and Termination of the American Revolution*, Vol. 1, 121-122, MO. Warren.

ADDITIONAL SOURCES

1. *A History of the United States*, Arthur Cecil Bining.
2. *The Growth of the United States*, Ralph Volney Harlow.
3. *The Oxford Companion to United States History*, edited by Paul S. Boyer.
4. *The Oxford History of the American People,* Samuel Eliot Morrison.
5. *The American Revolution*, American Heritage, Inc. Introduction by Bruce Cotton.
6. *History's Greatest Lies*, William Weir.
7. *Founding Fathers*, National Geographic.
8. *John Adams*, David McCullough.
9. *The British Are Coming, The War for America*, Rick Atkinson.
10. *The Adversaries, A Story of Boston and Bunker Hill*, by Ned Ryan.

ACTS/EVENTS PRECEDING THE AMERICAN REVOLUTION

1. Quartering (Billeting) Act — An amendment to the Mutiny Act of 1765 that required colonial governments to billet troops in inns, barns, and uninhabited houses when barracks were not available, as well as other provisions. This shifted the cost from English taxpayers to the colonists.

2. Molasses Act, 1733 — The law forced ship owners to smuggle molasses and sugar into the colonies from the French and Spanish West Indies rather than pay the high tax.

3. Sugar (or Revenue) Act, 1764 — In an attempt to stop smuggling, the tax was reduced, believing that colonists would be willing to pay a reduced tax rather than smuggle goods.

4. Currency Act, 1764 — In 1751, Parliament forbade any New England government to issue any more legal tender bills of credit. The Currency Act extended the prohibition to all other colonies.

5. Writs of Assistance, 1751, 1761, 1765 — Allowed customs officials to conduct arbitrary searches of homes and businesses to mitigate smuggling. The holder of the writ was not responsible for any damage during the search.

6. Stamp Act, 1765 — Required legal documents and official papers to be written on stamped paper, and stamps were to be affixed to pamphlets, newspapers, almanacs, playing cards, and dice when sold. This caused a loud response: "No taxation without representation." This was repealed on March 18, 1766, and replaced by the Declaratory Act, which stated that Britain had sole authority to make laws, etc. over the colonies.

7. Townshend Act, 1767 — Provided for a reorganization of the customs service in America. A Board of Commissioners of the Customs was established in Boston to supervise collection of duties.

8. Regulating Act (Tea Act), 1773 — Gave the East India Company (nearly insolvent) a monopoly of carrying tea to the colonies. American commerce and liberty were threatened.

9. Boston Tea Party, 1773 — A group of men dressed as Mohawk Indians threw tea overboard from the *Eleanor*, the *Dartmouth*, and the *Beaver*, which were tied up at Griffin's Wharf. The tea was valued at over nine thousand pounds. Some believe that Dr. Warren and members of the St. Andrews Masonic Lodge were involved.

10. Boston Port Act, 1773 — Closed the Port of Boston until the East India Company was compensated 9,000 pounds sterling for the tea destroyed by the Tea Party and moved the seat of colonial government to Salem until the Port of Boston was reopened.

11. Intolerable Acts (Coercive Act), 1774 – The Coercive Act, the Boston Port Act (March), the Massachusetts Government Act (May), the Administration of Justice Act (May), and the Quartering Act (June) were collectively referred to as the Intolerable Acts.

12. Boston Massacre, March 5, 1770 — A Patriot mob harassed a contingent of soldiers on guard outside of the State House. The troops fired, killing three, and two more later died of their wounds. Others wounded survived.

13. Quebec Act, 1774 – Extended the boundaries of Quebec south to the Ohio River and west to the Mississippi River. This took away lands already claimed and placed these lands within a new royal province. It granted the French colonists freedom of religion along the St. Lawrence Valley, which meant that Great Britain had sanctioned Catholicism in that part of America.

14. Suffolk Resolves, 1774 (written by Dr. Warren) —
    a. Called for an immediate stoppage of all trade with England, Ireland, and the West Indies.
    b. Urged all Americans to organize a militia for defense. Dr. Warren denounced England as "...the parricide which points the dagger to our bosoms..." and declared that the streets of Boston were "...thronged with military executioners..." and that the compact between George III and Massachusetts was "...totally wrecked, annulled and vacated."

ADDENDUM

The provincial losses at the Battle of Breed's Hill were listed as 139 killed, 278 wounded, and 36 missing. Another source recorded that approximately 3,500 colonial men were engaged in the fight with 115 killed, 305 wounded, and 30 taken prisoners. The number of British troops engaged were recorded to be about 4,000. Governor General Thomas Gage acknowledged a loss of 1,054: 226 killed and 828 wounded (Alexander Everett in his *Life of Joseph Warren* states that Colonel Swett listed details of the action in his *History of the Battle of Bunker Hill*). The battle began about 3 p.m. on June 17, 1775, and lasted about two hours. Major General Joseph Warren, M.D. was among the dead. His bullet wound to the head resulted in instantaneous death and would have occurred about 5:00 p.m. The account recorded in the official record in the Congress of Massachusetts states: "Among the dead was Major General Joseph Warren, a man whose memory will be endeared to his countrymen and to the worthy in every part of the world, so long as virtue and valor are esteemed among mankind."

The Continental Congress resolved that "public provisions" would be made for the education of the Warren children. Joseph and Richard died in their twenties and had never married. Elizabeth, born in 1765, married General Arnold Wells in 1785 (age 20). She died in Boston on July 26, 1804, at age 39 (without issue). Joseph was born in 1768, and graduated from Harvard in 1786; he died suddenly on April 2, 1790, while visiting the home of his uncle Ebenezer. Mary was twice married. Her first husband was Mr. Lyman of Northampton. She lost all her children by this marriage. Her second husband was Judge Richard E. Newcomb of Greenfield, Massachusetts. Judge Newcomb stated in a letter dated April 14, 1843, "My late wife, Mary, was the youngest and only surviving child of the late General Joseph Warren. She died on February 7, 1826; leaving an only child, a son, who bares the name of his grandfather, Joseph Warren. He is an attorney-at-law, and now lives at Springfield, in this state. He, with the exception of his two children, is the only descendant, in a direct line, of him who fell on Bunker Hill. Both of these children are living. One is the wife of Dr. Buckminster Brown, and resides in Boston. Richard, according to the letter of Samuel Adams, born about 1772, was engaged in the mercantile business in Alexandria; returned to Boston; and died in the home of his uncle, Dr. John Warren, at the age of twenty-one."

The "Bible" that Dr. Warren always carried in his pocket was actually the Book of Psalms. It is now in the Massachusetts Historical Society. The book is 3-1/2 by 5 inches, bound in leather with a fleur de lis embossed in gold. One of the earliest versions printed in English, it was published in Geneva Switzerland in 1559, and was more than 200 years old when Dr. Warren carried it. The book was purchased in England in early 1778 by a minister who bought it from a British soldier who claimed that he had taken it off the body of Dr. Joseph Warren immediately after the Battle of Bunker Hill. The minister then, several weeks before his own death, sent the book to Rev. William Gordon, the historian, then living in Roxbury, Massachusetts, with instructions that it go to Warren's family. The signature "J. Warren" was on page 162 at Psalm 68. It was identified as Dr. Warren's signature by his niece. (Brown, *Stories About General Warren*, 78-80.)

Other items exist that some claim to have been Dr. Warren's: a Latin grammar book, 1720 edition; a ceremonial masonic apron; a military vest; the fatal bullet; Warren's sword; a grandfather clock; and a chair.

Following the Breed's Hill battle, the remainder of the day, throughout the night, and the following day was spent by both sides retrieving their wounded and then burying their dead. Immediately after the battle, "...a small group of seething redcoats circled the body of Warren..." and since "...he was the hallmark of everything the British soldiers despised,... they vented their fury upon him" (*Founding Martyr*).

"What was left of Warren remained on the field overnight. He was buried hastily in a trench on the morning after the battle (Sunday, June 18, 1775), his mutilated corpse tossed unceremoniously into a shallow ditch in a mass grave of slain and murdered patriots." Lt.

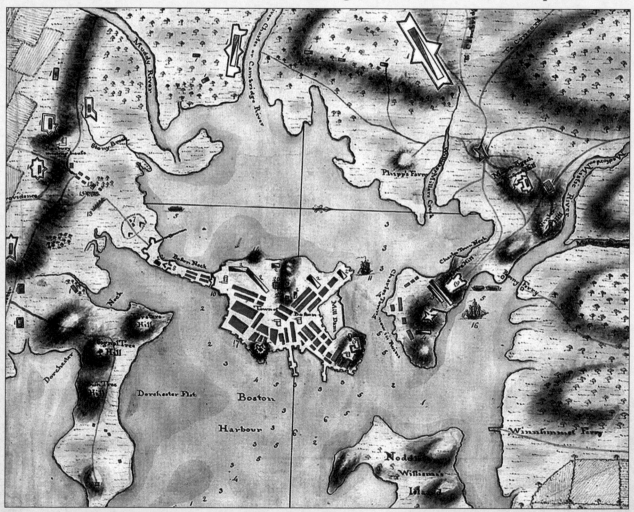

Drawn by a British soldier in the early months of 1776, this map details Boston Harbor and the damage done to Charlestown, which was burned by the American colonists on January 8. The British would be forced to evacuate the city after George Washington captured Dorchester Heights in March 1776.

Walter Laurie in charge of the burial detail wrote, "I found Dr. Warren among the slain and stuffed the scoundrel with another rebel, into one hole, and there he and his seditious principles may remain." (Ibid.) Governor General Thomas Hutchinson, who had known Warren for years, both personally and professionally, firmly believed that "...if he had lived, [Warren] bid as fair as any man to advance himself to the summit of political as well as military affairs and to become the Cromwell of North America." Former Chief Justice of the Massachusetts Superior Court, felt that had Warren lived, [General George] Washington would have "...remained in obscurity." (Ibid.)

The Bunker Hill battle finally achieved the break with the Crown that Warren had long sought. King George III declared the colonists to be in "...open and avowed rebellion, by arraying themselves in a hostile manner, to withstand the execution of the law, and traitorously preparing, ordering, and levying war against us." The rebellion had indeed become a war!

Colonial troops under the command of General Washington forced the British evacuation of Boston on March 17, 1776, nine months to the day after the Battle of Bunker Hill. John Warren, M.D., Joseph Warren's younger brother, was one of the first to be granted permission by General Washington to enter Charlestown. Four days later on March 21, 1776, he began his search for Dr. Warren's body. On April 4, John and his brother Ebenezer found his grave. His unclothed remains were found in a shallow grave beneath a "...person buried in trousers." His body was horribly decomposed, but was identified by his brothers by two artificial teeth in his left upper jaw that had been fashioned for him by Paul Revere, the silversmith, who accompanied the Warren brothers to the gravesite.

After the exhumed remains were placed in an elegant coffin, they were removed from Charlestown to the State House at the head of State Street. Dr. Warren's remains lay in state for several days. "On April 8, they were carried on a funeral bier — draped with a pall — by the Hon. General Ward, Brigadier General Frye, Dr. Morgan, Col. Gridley, the Hon. Mr. Gill, and Mercy's father, John Scollay. A procession of several hundred mourners and a detachment of Continental soldiers moved in somber unison to King's Chapel. Col. Phinney's regiment marched first with drums and fifes in mourning, then the Free Masons, the casket, the family, friends, and town's people. All the usual Masonic ceremonies were performed for their Grand Master. Inside King's Chapel, a moving funeral dirge was played. Warren's Masonic brother and friend Perez Morton, said to be one of the most talented writers in Massachusetts, delivered the eulogy. Dr. Samuel Cooper preached the sermon, then kneeled over the remains of his dear friend and prayed. Warren's mother, Mary Warren, and Warren's children were a part of the funeral procession as it arrived at the Old Granary Burial Grounds, where her son and their father was laid to rest in the George Richards Minot tomb in Boston, April 8, 1776.

Nearly half a century later in 1825, Dr. Joseph Warren's remains were located in the Minot tomb by his nephew, John Collins Warren, M.D. The remains were placed in a hardwood box and moved to the Warren Tomb in St. Paul's Church in Boston. A silver plate on the box had the following inscription: "In this tomb are deposited the earthly remains of Major-General Joseph Warren, who was killed in the Battle of Bunker Hill on June 17, 1775."

His remains were again disinterred by John C. Warren, M.D. on August 3, 1855, and retained in his home for one year. (During this year, the skull was photographed.) John Col-

Dr. John Collins Warren with his hand on a random skull, daguerreotype, ca. 1849.

lins Warren died May 4, 1856. His son, Jonathan Mason Warren, M.D. reburied Joseph Warren, M.D's remains for the final time in the Forest Hills Cemetery in Roxbury, Massachusetts, on August 8, 1856.

Major General Joseph Warren, M.D.'s mother, Mary Stevens Warren, died in 1803. Several Boston papers reported in their obituary notices of January 20: "At Roxbury, on Friday last, Mrs. Mary Warren, aged ninety. Few among the sons and daughters of Adam have attained so advanced an age, fewer still with faculties so unimpaired, very few with a character so unspotted. An unshaken confidence in the rectitude of the Divine government rendered her firm and serene through every stage of life. Of the cup of adversity she had sometimes drank deeply; but the religion of Jesus was her never-failing support. It was this that prompted to the exercise of universal beneficence; it was this which heightened her relish for social intercourse and enjoyment; and the cheerfulness it inspired, together with an uncommon strength of mind, made her, at a period of life which is usually but labor and sorrow, the welcome companion of the young and the aged. And it was this which at last enabled her to meet the approach of death, for which she, at that interesting hour, expressed herself that she had been all her life preparing, without a terror and without a groan." (*Life and Times of Joseph Warren*, pp. 8-9, Frothingham.)

Headstone of Mercy Scollay, Vine Lake Cemetery, Medfield, Massachusetts.

William Cushing, later an U.S. Supreme Court Justice (Feb. 2, 1790-Sept. 13, 1810), had been one of Joseph Warren's (III) teachers at Roxbury Latin School. He was one of the first five Justices on the Supreme Court. President George Washington nominated him to the court on Sept. 24, 1789, and later nominated him to be Chief Justice in 1796, but Cushing declined.

Very little is known about Miss Mercy Scollay's life prior to the Revolutionary War. She and her parents, father John Scollay and mother, also Mercy Scollay, and her four sisters were patients of Dr. Warren. After Elizabeth Warren died in 1773, she and Dr. Warren gradually became close friends, and probably less than a year before the Battle of Breed's Hill, they became engaged. There were five Scollay children, all girls, four living to adulthood: Deborah (b. 1736), Mercy (b. 1741), Mary (b. and d. 1752), Priscilla (b. 1755), and Mary (b. 1760). Both Deborah and Priscilla married Melvill[e]s. (Priscilla became the grandmother of novelist Herman Melville.) Mercy went to live with her baby sister Mary Scollay Prentiss in Medfield, Massachusetts in 1797.

Mercy was a writer and poet and a Daughter of Liberty. Her first poem was printed in Isaiah Thomas' *Royal American Magazine* in June 1774. Ninety letters written by Miss Scollay are located at the Cambridge Historical Society in Cambridge, Massachusetts. Forman included in his book, *Dr. Joseph Warren: The Boston Tea Party, Bunker Hill and the Birth of American Liberty*, an elegy written by Mercy after the death of her fiancé. It is a twenty quatrain poem to his memory.

No picture exists of Mercy. A miniature painting by John Singleton Copley was exhibited at a Boston Daughters of the American Revolution in 1894, but it cannot now be found. Copley's portrait, "Lady in a Blue Dress" in the Terra Foundation Museum in Chicago is believed to be Mercy Scollay at age twenty-two.

When Joseph Warren (III) left Boston and his practice of medicine/surgery to avoid capture by the British, Warren asked Mercy to "...write for the revolutionary cause..." and "...to care for his children.." if he should die in the war. Frothingham praised Mercy Scollay, "Miss Scollay deserves the greatest praise for her charge; and her affection for their deceased father prompts her to exert her utmost to inculcate in the minds of these children those principals which may render them Worthy of the relation they stood in to him" (*Life and Times of Joseph Warren*).

John Warren, M.D., Joseph Warren, M.D.'s younger brother, founded the Harvard Medical School and was the first professor of surgery, and his son, John Collins Warren, M.D founded the Massachusetts General Hospital and the Massachusetts Medical Association.

—Jerry W. Martin, M.D.

"...first great martyr in the great cause."
—Daniel Webster

"...Freedom wept!"
—Abigail Adams

"They, the Bostonians, had received a nation from their fathers, and they proposed to make it a great nation."
—Van Wyck Brooks
The Flowering of New England

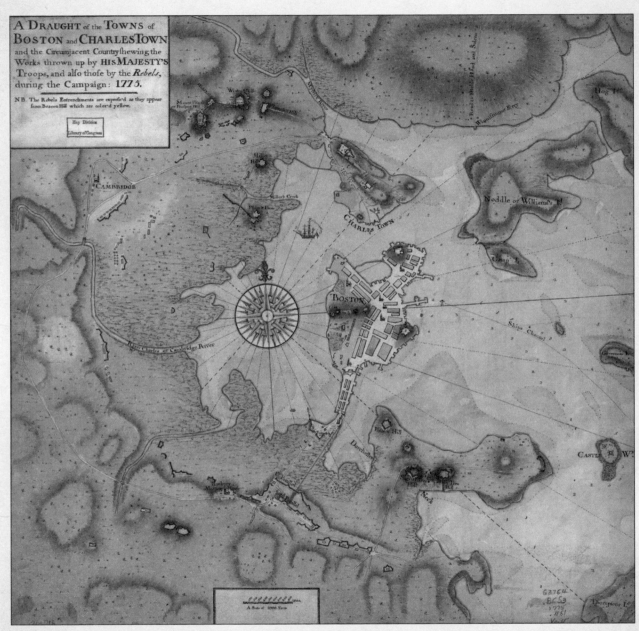

Created by a loyal subject in 1775, this is described as "a draught of the towns of Boston and Charles Town and the circumjacent country showing the works thrown up by His Majesty's troops, and also those by the rebels, during the campaign."

Joseph Warren

2nd President of the Massachusetts Provincial Congress

In Office
May 2, 1775 – June 17, 1775

Preceded by
John Adams

Succeeded by
James Warren

Died
June 17, 1775 (aged 34)
Breed's Hill, Charlestown, Province of Massachusetts Bay, British America

Cause of Death
Killed in Action

Resting Place
Forest Hills Cemetery

Spouse
Elizabeth Hooten

Relations
Mercy Scollay (fiancée)

Children
Elizabeth, Joseph, Mary, and Richard

Education
Roxbury Latin School

Alma Mater
Harvard College

Occupation
Physician

Military Service
Allegiance to Massachusetts, United Colonies

Branch of Service
Massachusetts Patriot Militia

Years of Service
1775

Rank
Militiaman, Major General

Battles/Wars
American Revolutionary War
Massachusetts Campaign
Battles of Lexington and Concord
Siege of Boston
Battle of Bunker Hill

Surrounded by thirteen stars on a field of blue, a proud eagle adorns an early iteration of the American flag, created ca. 1781.

UNION AND LIBERTY

FLAG of the heroes who left us their glory,
Borne through their battle-fields' thunder and flame,
Blazoned in song and illumined in story,
Wave o'er us all who inherit their fame!

 Up with our banner bright,
 Sprinkled with starry light,
 Spread its fair emblems from mountain to shore,
 While through the sounding sky
 Loud rings the Nation's cry,
 UNION AND LIBERTY! ONE EVERMORE!

Light of our firmament, guide of our Nation,
Pride of her children, and honored afar,
Let the wide beams of thy full constellation
Scatter each cloud that would darken a star!

 Up with our banner bright,
 Sprinkled with starry light,
 Spread its fair emblems from mountain to shore,
 While through the sounding sky
 Loud rings the Nation's cry,
 UNION AND LIBERTY! ONE EVERMORE!

Empire unsceptred! what foe shall assail thee,
Bearing the standard of Liberty's van?
Think not the God of thy fathers shall fail thee,
Striving with men for the birthright of man!

 Up with our banner bright,
 Sprinkled with starry light,
 Spread its fair emblems from mountain to shore,
 While through the sounding sky
 Loud rings the Nation's cry,
 UNION AND LIBERTY! ONE EVERMORE!

Yet if, by madness and treachery blighted,
Dawns the dark hour when the sword thou must draw,
Then with the arms of thy millions united,
Smite the bold traitors to Freedom and Law!

    Up with our banner bright,
    Sprinkled with starry light,
    Spread its fair emblems from mountain to shore,
    While through the sounding sky
    Loud rings the Nation's cry,
    UNION AND LIBERTY! ONE EVERMORE!

Lord of the Universe! shield us and guide us,
Trusting Thee always, through shadow and sun!
Thou hast united us, who shall divide us?
Keep us, oh keep us the MANY IN ONE!

    Up with our banner bright,
    Sprinkled with starry light,
    Spread its fair emblems from mountain to shore,
    While through the sounding sky
    Loud rings the Nation's cry,
    UNION AND LIBERTY! ONE EVERMORE!

—Oliver Wendell Holmes, M.D., 1861

Counties Named for Joseph Warren

State	Population per Recent Census*	Date Named
North Carolina	20,972	1779
Georgia	5,834	1793
Pennsylvania	41,815	1795
Kentucky	113,792	1796
Ohio	212,693	1803
Tennessee	39,839	1807
Mississippi	48,773	1809
New York	65,707	1813
New Jersey	108,692	1824
Missouri	32,513	1833
Virginia	37,575	1836
Iowa	46,225	1846

*U.S. census figures for 2010

Top Fifteen Frequently Used Eastern Massachusetts Street and Place Names*

Rank	Name	Uses	Type
1	Washington	188	Person
2	Lincoln	182	Person
3	Adams	147	Persons and family
4	Franklin	142	Person
5	Warren	131	Person
6	Union	123	Political Construct
7	King**	109	Office/Monarchical, Political Construct
8	Colonial	96	Political Construct
9	Liberty	93	Political Construct
10	Columbus	83	Person
11	Bradford	88	Person and Family
12	Parker	86	Person
13	Plymouth	83	Place
14	Concord	77	Place
15	Hancock	64	Person

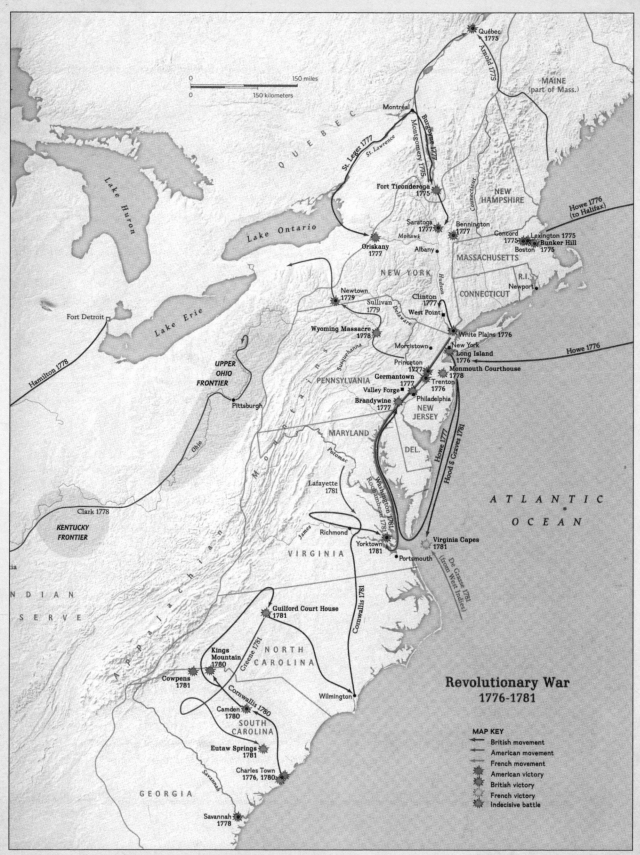

Revolutionary War
1776-1781

MAP KEY

→ British movement
← American movement
→ French movement
✳ American victory
✳ British victory
✳ French victory
✳ Indecisive battle

General map of the Revolutionary War.

American Revolution map of Boston

This drawing shows the view from a British redoubt on Beacon Hill, with cannon and soldiers in the foreground. The caption identifies prominent features, such as the Mystic River, North Boston.

Sometimes called the headquarters of the Revolution, the Green Dragon public house in Boston's North End was often used by Paul Revere, John Hancock, and other patriots as a meeting place to plan operations against the British.

A paper Virginia note from 1775 worth 15 pence.

A $50 note …
American currency dated 1778.

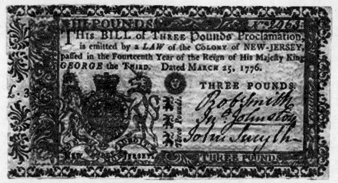

A three-pound New Jersey note dated 1776.

South Carolina colonial note worth $70.

Two 1779 certificates using "secret" marks to help distinguish genuine bills from counterfeit ones.

The front and back of a British halfpenny coin dated 1775.

INSTRUMENTS OF BATTLE

Revolutionary-era musket from Fort Ticonderoga

A powder horn from
Fort Ticonderoga

Colonial musket balls with
nails embedded in them

A drum believed to have been used
at the Battle of Bunker Hill.

A 66-caliber smoothbore flintlock pistol
made in Annapolis, Maryland, in the
early days of the Revolution.

A Revolutionary-era cartridge
box and belt, worn at the
soldier's right hip.

A Colonial saber from Fort Ticonderoga in New York

CONTINENTAL UNIFORMS

An American officer's cocked hat, commonly worn in the 18th century.

Embroidered mitre cap, worn by the Governors Foot Guard of Connecticut, ca. 1774.

American Light Dragoon helmet made of heavy leather with brass trimmings and horsehair crest.

The triangular-style hat, popular during the 18th century

Regimental coat that belonged to Lt. Col. Benjamin Holden of Col. Ephraim Doolittle's Minute-Men's Regiment

Striped linen waistcoat worn by Lt. Col. William Ledyard of the Connecticut Militia

Continental Army uniform coat worn by Col. Peter Gansevoort Jr. of the Third Regiment of the New York Continental Line

A wooden canteen used by a New Jersey soldier.

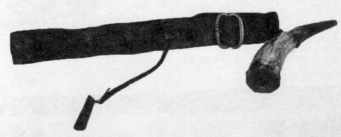

Belt with powder horn carried by an American rifleman.

GEORGE WASHINGTON

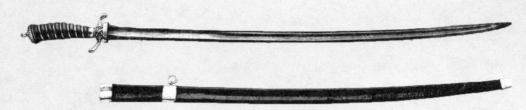

George Washington's battle sword and scabbard

Washington's pocket fishing case, containing hooks, fishing lines, and other supplies.

Canteen made from leather, wood, linen, and copper.

A portable writing case used by George Washington.

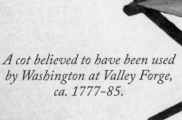

A cot believed to have been used by Washington at Valley Forge, ca. 1777–85.

Washington wore this uniform to the Constitutional Convention in 1787.

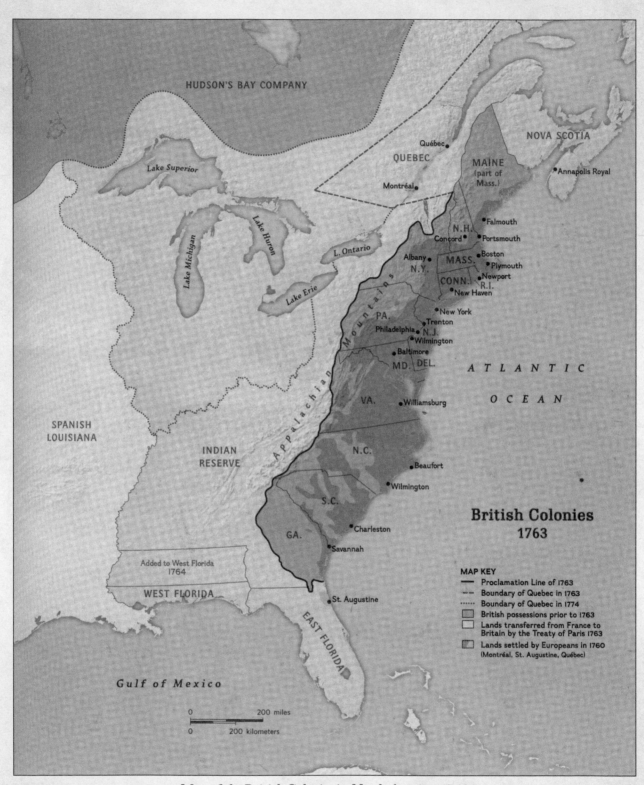

Map of the British Colonies in North America, 1763.

HUDSON'S BAY COMPANY

NOVA SCOTIA

Québec
QUEBEC
•Annapolis Royal
MAINE
(part of
Mass.)

Montréal

Lake Superior

Lake Michigan

Lake Huron

L. Ontario

Lake Erie

N.H.
•Falmouth
Concord• •Portsmouth
Albany•   •Boston
MASS.
N.Y.   •Plymouth
CONN.   •Newport
•New Haven   R.I.

•New York

PA.
•Trenton
Philadelphia• N.J.
•Wilmington
•Baltimore
MD. DEL.

ATLANTIC

OCEAN

VA.
•Williamsburg

SPANISH
LOUISIANA

INDIAN
RESERVE

N.C.

•Beaufort
•Wilmington

S.C.

GA.
•Charleston

•Savannah

British Colonies
1763

Added to West Florida
1764

WEST FLORIDA

•St. Augustine

EAST FLORIDA

Gulf of Mexico

MAP KEY
—— Proclamation Line of 1763
–·– Boundary of Quebec in 1763
···· Boundary of Quebec in 1774
▨ British possessions prior to 1763
▢ Lands transferred from France to
   Britain by the Treaty of Paris 1763
▨ Lands settled by Europeans in 1760
   (Montréal, St. Augustine, Québec)

0 ____ 200 miles
0 ____ 200 kilometers

Appalachian Mountains

Land Claims of the Thirteen Colonies

The 1763 Treaty of Paris ended the Seven Years' War that had pitted France and Spain against Britain. The conflict engulfed territories and empires worldwide, from the Americas to Europe to India and the Philippines. To the British colonists of North America, it was known as the French and Indian War.

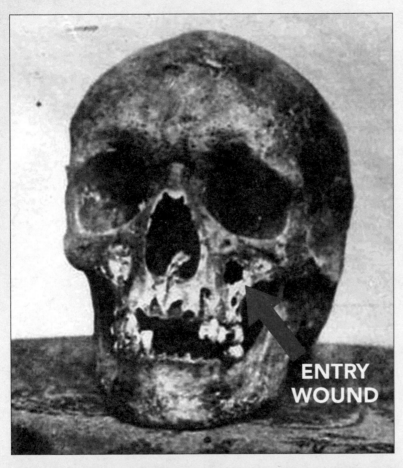

ENTRY WOUND

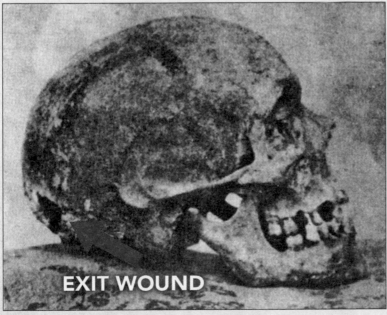

EXIT WOUND

Joseph Warren's skull, both front and side views, showing the entrance and exit holes for the shot that killed him. An unsubstantiated rumor circulated that the British officer who had Dr. Warren in his musket sights chose not to shoot him, since they were acquainted; in fact, he had been a patient of Dr. Warren's. His aide then unexpectedly grabbed the officer's pistol and fired, killing Dr. Warren instantly. Whether true or not, it is obviously untrue that Dr. Warren was shot by a musket "behind the ear". As pictured, the entrance and exit wounds on his skull were much smaller, as from a smaller caliber weapon such as a pistol. The bullet entered the left maxillary sinus, passed through the midbrain and exited the right occipital area on the back of the skull. This seems to substantiate the rumor noted above.

Warren's clock,
Scottish Rite Masonic Museum and Library,
Lexington, Massachusetts.

Bunker Hill monument etching,
ca. 1843.

Patrick Henry, 1736–1799
Energetic, erratic, and persuasive, Patrick Henry was a self-taught lawyer who early on in the struggle with Britain captured the public imagination with his fiery rhetoric. At the First Continental Congress, he declared, "I am not a Virginian, but an American," yet his national role ended after one session of the Second Continental Congress. Returning to Virginia, he continued to press for revolution and military preparedness. In 1776 he became the first elected governor of the state, and over the course of his life served five terms as Virginia governor. After independence, Henry became increasingly wary of a strong central government and the Constitution, calling its objectives "extremely pernicious, impolitic, and dangerous." In the early years of the Republic, he opposed the ideas of Madison, Jefferson, and particularly Hamilton, but continued to believe in the union of states. In 1799 he was elected delegate to the state legislature, but died at his home, Red Hill, before he could take his seat.

Archibald MacNeal Willard's famous painting "The Spirit of '76" is also known by the nickname, "Yankee Doodle."

ABOUT THE AUTHOR

Jerry W. Martin, M.D., was born in Providence (Webster County), Kentucky, on November 28, 1935, to Charles R. Martin, Jr. and Rosena Playl Martin. He graduated from Providence High School in 1954 and continued his education at Vanderbilt University in 1954-55 (Sigma Nu), B.S. from Western Kentucky State College, 1958, and M.D. at University of Louisville School of Medicine in 1963 (Alpha Kappa Kappa).

He married Jimmie D. Hobgood on December 18, 1955. They have two daughters: Melissa Martin Johnson, RN and Mary Elizabeth Martin, B.S., D.V.M.; a son, Charles Stanley Martin, B.S., B.A., M.A., J.D.; one grandchild, Elizabeth Johnson Hathaway, B.A.; and one great-grandchild, Sarah Elizabeth Hathaway.

He was drafted from private practice in 1966. After attending the Medical Field Service School in 1966 at Brooke Army Medical Center, Fort Sam Houston, San Antonio, Texas, he was assigned to the 18th Surgical Hospital (MA), Pleiku, Pleiku

Photograph by Tom Brown

Province, Republic of (South) Vietnam (Central Highlands), June 1966-June 1967. Upon returning to the U.S., he was Director of the Out Patient Clinic, U.S. Army Hospital, Fort Campbell, Kentucky (July 5 to December 11, 1967).

He worked in private practice of Family Medicine in Bowling Green, Warren County, Kentucky from 1964 to 2002, he served as Warren County Medical Society President (1971-72); KAFP (President [1985-86] and Doctor of the Year [1990]); Charter Diplomat ABFP; Warren County Board of Health (1973-80); Chief of Staff, BG-WC Hospital (1970-71); President of Staff (1976-77) and Chairman, Board of Trustees, Greenview Hospital (1978-79); Board of Directors, Warren County Chapter, American Heart Association (1981-97); KMA Board of Trustees (1987-93); Board of Directors of KEMPAC (1987-92); AAFP Bylaws Committee (1993-96), Chairman (1996); Delegate to AAFP (1992-98); Fellow, Royal Society of Medicine (1992-); Associate Professor, U of L Dept. of Family Medicine; AAFP Delegate to AMA (1996-2008); WKU Team Physician (1968 2002); Physicians Recognition Award (19170-2006); AAGP and Founding Fellow, AAFP; Charter Member, American College of Emergency Physicians (1970); Life Member, KMA and AMA.

Member of First Baptist Church since 1964, Deacon since 1968 (Chairman 1996 and 2002); Chairman, Committee to Commemorate 175th Anniversary (1993); History and Archives Committee (1975-2003), Chairman (1995-2003); Former Member, BG-WC Jaycees and Rotary Club; Member: Kentucky Historical Society; Filson Club; Kentucky Ornithological Society; Photography Society of America (1965-), Area Representative (1976-88), District Representative (1988-93); and a Member of EQB Literary Club (1982-).

Other Books by
JERRY W. MARTIN, M.D.

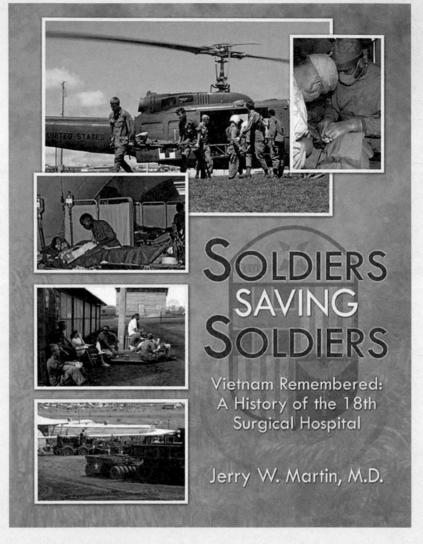

Soldiers Saving Soldiers is the story of the 18th Surgical Hospital and the doctors, nurses, medics and support personnel who were stationed at Pleiku, South Vietnam during the Vietnam War. In particular, it centers on the experiences of Dr. Jerry W. Martin, who stationed there from June 1966-June 1967.

Part combat hospital and part medical clinic for Vietnamese and Montagnard villagers, the 18th Surgical Hospital served as a vital lifeline and saved the lives of thousands of American servicemen, enemy combatants and local families throughout the Vietnam War. Like their fellow countrymen who fought the war, the men and women of the 18th Surgical Hospital have been forever changed by their experiences in Vietnam, both good and bad. The book also presents the entire history of the unit, from its origins in 1928 through World War II, and then from reactivation in Vietnam through 1971. In addition, Dr. Martin presents the day-to-day life of a field surgeon with a look at dozens of surgical procedures and their outcomes (with detailed full-color case photographs, plus nearly 500 photographs of people and places throughout Vietnam.

Soldiers Saving Soldiers is an excellent book for veterans, their families and military historians, and also presents excellent case studies for medical professionals and modern-day field surgeons.

In *Symbols and Myths of Medicine*, Dr. Jerry W. Martin explores what early men believed about medicine and healing, and how ancient symbols and myths evolved through time. In particular, the book details the medicinal practices and symbols of Greek, Roman and other cultures, and explains how these symbols may still be found in the medical community today.

INDEX

Endnotes and Sources not included in index.